Preventing Mold-Related Problems in the Indoor Workplace

A Guide for Building Owners, Managers and Occupants

U.S. Department of Labor

Occupational Safety and Health Administration

OSHA 3304-04N
2006

Contents

Introduction

This guide provides basic information about mold, mold sources, and building-related illnesses. Brief discussions are included on building design considerations for healthy indoor air, as well as building evaluation and sampling for mold. However, detailed information about indoor air quality diagnostic studies (e.g., normal vs. abnormal levels) and the design and execution of exposure sampling strategies is not included as this information is beyond the scope of this initiative. For approaches to remediation of moldy areas and the appropriate response based on the degree of the contamination, the reader should consult OSHA's Safety and Health Information Bulletin (SHIB 03-10-10) "A Brief Guide to Mold in the Workplace" (1). Additional information on mold is available through OSHA's "Molds and Fungi" safety and health topics webpage at http://www.osha.gov/SLTC/molds/index.html, which contains a collection of hyperlinks to various sources of information regarding mold.

Background

In 1994, OSHA published in the *Federal Register* a comprehensive proposed rule on indoor air quality (IAQ) that addressed adverse health effects attributable to environmental tobacco smoke (ETS) and other indoor pollutants, including bioaerosols (59 FR 15968). During the IAQ rulemaking, the Agency received comments and scientific and technical information on indoor mold exposures associated with building-related illnesses (BRIs). While the IAQ proposed rule was withdrawn in its entirety in December 2001 (66 FR 64946), the Agency retained the voluminous docket (consisting of approximately 120,000 documents), which contains valuable information on ETS and other indoor pollutants, such as chemicals, bacteria, and molds.

In preparing this guide OSHA has reviewed the IAQ docket and recent scientific literature pertaining to mold exposures.[1] As a result of this review, it is clear that the entrance of water (i.e., incursion) into buildings that are damaged, poorly designed, or improperly maintained, is the main source of mold-associated building-related illness. Consequently, the focus of the review was directed toward preventive measures to reduce potential environments for mold growth at the source.

The purpose of this guide is to help owners, managers, and occupants understand and prevent building-related illnesses associated with mold problems in offices and other indoor workplaces.[2] It is not the intent of this guide to address the special considerations of building designers, developers, and similar building professionals; however, they may find certain general information helpful. In addition, health care professionals, maintenance workers, custodians, and others who have a role in the prevention and correction (i.e., remediation) of mold problems in buildings may derive benefit from the information and recommendations outlined here.

---

[1] See Methods Section of this document for further details regarding the process used to review the scientific literature and analyze the IAQ docket information concerning mold exposures.

[2] Building-related illnesses discussed in this guide are limited to those illnesses that arise in nonindustrial, nonresidential buildings.

Overview

Mold

Molds are the most common forms of fungi found on the earth. Fungi are classified as neither plants nor animals, and include yeasts, mildews, puffballs, and mushrooms (2). Most molds reproduce through the formation of spores, tiny microscopic cells that float through the indoor and outdoor air on a continual basis (3). We are all exposed to mold spores in the air we breathe on a daily basis, both indoors and outdoors. When mold spores land on a moist surface indoors, they may begin to grow and digest the surface. Left unchecked, molds can eventually destroy the surfaces they grow on (3). Molds can be any color.

Molds, their fragments, and metabolic by-products have been associated with adverse health effects. Some diseases are known to be caused by specific molds. However, in many occupational settings health conditions suspected to be mold-related cannot be linked to a specific mold as the only possible cause. In a well-known case an initial finding that *Stachybotrys chartarum* (also known as *S. atra*) was linked to acute pulmonary hemorrhage/hemosiderosis in infants living in a water-damaged environment in Cleveland, Ohio was subsequently disproved (4).

Where molds are found

Molds are found almost everywhere in our environment, both outdoors and indoors. Their spores float continually in the air we breathe. Molds can grow on just about any substance, as long as moisture and oxygen are available. Mold growth may occur when excessive moisture accumulates in buildings or on building materials including carpet, ceiling tile, insulation, paper, wallboard, wood, surfaces behind wallpaper, or in heating, ventilation, and air conditioning (HVAC) systems (3, 5).

The causes of molds in buildings

It is impossible to eliminate all molds and mold spores in the indoor environment. However, moisture control is the most important strategy for reducing indoor mold growth.

Common sources of moisture in buildings include plumbing, roof, and window leaks; flooding; condensation on cold surfaces (e.g., pipe sweating); poorly maintained drain pans; and wet foundations due to landscaping or gutters that direct water into or under the building. Water vapor from unvented or poorly vented kitchens, showers, combustion appliances, or steam pipes can also create conditions that promote mold growth (3).

Mold can grow wherever there is dampness. Damp or wet building materials and furnishings should be cleaned and dried within 24 to 48 hours to prevent the growth of mold (1, 3).

Why building owners and managers need to be concerned about mold

Building owners and managers, among others, make numerous decisions about design, operation, and maintenance throughout the life cycles of their buildings.

Structural damage to buildings from mold growth is one concern for building owners and managers. If sources of moisture are not controlled, mold, which is always present to some degree, can spread and cause damage to building materials, finishes, and furnishings. Additionally, some molds can cause structural damage to wood (6).

Structural damage, however, is not the only concern. Large amounts of mold growth in buildings can create odors and may trigger health effects, such as allergic reactions, in some individuals. Illnesses that are associated with mold exposures in buildings have been evaluated in this document. The results of this evaluation indicate that, in general, the relationships between poor indoor air quality due to the presence of mold and building-related illnesses (BRIs) are unclear. This stems, in part, from the lack of standardized and meaningful methods by which to measure mold exposures and their effects on occupants. However, widespread symptoms related to a building can lead to environmental investigation, mitigation activities, relocation of occupants, and loss of tenants or property value. Problems that follow an onset of health complaints associated with buildings may impact employers located in buildings and sometimes the building owners who may have to bear high costs to resolve the underlying issues.

Information on indoor mold exposures is constantly changing. As new and critical information develops, building professionals and occupants who access the information will be able to incorporate the information into successful resolution of any existing building mold problems (7).

Building-related illnesses (BRIs)

The term building-related illness (BRI) is used to describe illnesses that are characterized by objective clinical findings related to specific exposures in the indoor environment. Building-related illnesses (BRIs) are diagnosed by evaluation of signs and symptoms by physicians or other licensed health care professionals. Mold-related BRIs result from mold contamination that has occurred in buildings under specific conditions. All BRIs are preventable by eliminating and controlling the conditions that can lead to the harmful exposures.

How Sick Building Syndrome (SBS) differs from BRI

Terms such as Sick Building Syndrome (SBS) have been used to describe situations in which building occupants experience a variety of symptoms that, unlike BRIs, appear to be linked to time spent in a building, but no specific illness or cause can be identified (8). Symptoms often disappear after occupants leave the building (9).

BRIs linked to mold exposure

The health effects of concern from exposure to mold contamination in an indoor environment can be common allergic BRIs such as allergic rhinitis, allergic asthma, and hypersensitivity pneumonitis (also called extrinsic allergic alveolitis) (10, 11), and infections such as histoplasmosis and cryptococcosis. Mycotoxins can also produce toxin-mediated adverse health effects. The following discussions of selected mold-related BRIs are not intended to be comprehensive, i.e., the descriptions do not include diagnostic tests or medical treatments. Rather, the discussions are informational and focused on common BRIs.

Building-Related Illnesses

Health effects that can be caused by mold

Most people experience no health effects from exposure to the molds present in indoor or outdoor air. However, some individuals with underlying health conditions may be more sensitive to molds. For example, individuals who have other allergies or existing respiratory conditions such as asthma, sinusitis, or other lung diseases may be more easily affected. Similarly, persons who have a weakened immune system tend to be more sensitive to molds. A person's immune system can be weakened if the individual has conditions such as pregnancy, diabetes, autoimmune disease, leukemia or AIDS; or if the individual is recovering from recent surgery or receiving chemotherapy or long-term treatment with steroids; or if the individual is the recipient of a recent organ or bone marrow transplant. In addition, infants, children, and the elderly have been shown to be more susceptible to health problems attributable to molds (1, 5, 9).

The most common health effects associated with mold exposure include allergic reactions similar to common pollen or animal allergies (5). Symptoms include sneezing, runny nose, eye irritation, coughing, congestion, aggravation of asthma, and skin rash (1, 3). These symptoms are also common reactions to other agents that cause allergies, and it is not always possible to single out the specific cause. More severe health reactions, such as hypersensitivity pneumonitis, can occur in susceptible individuals.

The three types of adverse health effects in humans caused by mold are allergy, infection, and toxin-mediated conditions (12). Further discussion of these health effects is provided in Appendix A of this document.

Preventive Maintenance

Preventing mold growth in occupied areas

The key to mold prevention is moisture control. The most important initial step in prevention is a visual inspection. Regular checks of the building envelope and drainage systems should be made to assure that they are in working order. Identify and, to the extent possible, eliminate sources of dampness, high humidity, and moisture to prevent mold growth. Wet or damp spots and wet, non-moldy materials should be cleaned and dried as soon as possible (preferably within 24 to 48 hours of discovery).

Moisture due to condensation may be prevented by increasing the surface temperature of the material where condensation is occurring, or by reducing the moisture level in the air (humidity). To increase the material's surface temperature, insulate it from the colder area or increase air circulation of warmer air. To reduce the moisture level in the air, repair leaks, increase ventilation (if outside air is cold and dry) or dehumidify (if outside air is warm and humid). Indoor relative humidity should be maintained below 70% (25-60%, if possible) (3).

All buildings should be checked routinely for water leaks, problem seals around doors and windows, and visible mold in moist or damp parts of the building. Any conditions that could be causes of mold growth should be corrected to prevent future mold problems.

Other prevention tips include venting moisture-generating appliances, such as dryers, to the outside where possible; venting kitchens (cooking areas) and bathrooms according to local code requirements; providing adequate drainage around buildings and sloping the ground away from the building foundations; and pinpointing areas where leaks have occurred, identifying the causes, and taking preventive action to ensure that they do not reoccur (3).

Preventing mold and bacterial growth in the building's ventilation system

Ventilation systems should be checked regularly, particularly for damp filters and overall cleanliness (1). A preventive maintenance plan should be put into place for each major component of the building's ventilation system. Contact your equipment supplier or manufacturer for recommended maintenance schedules and operations and maintenance manuals. Components that are exposed to water (e.g., drainage pans, coils, cooling towers, and humidifiers) require scrupulous maintenance to prevent microbial

growth and the entry of undesired microorganisms or chemicals into the indoor air stream (8).

Cleaning the building's air ducts

Air duct cleaning generally refers to the cleaning of various heating and cooling system components of forced air systems (13). The components of these systems may become contaminated with mold if moisture is present within the system, resulting in the potential release of mold spores throughout the building.

All components of the system must be cleaned. Failure to clean a component of a contaminated system can result in re-contamination of the entire system. Water-damaged or contaminated porous materials in the ductwork or other air handling system components should be removed and replaced (1, 8, 13). Ventilation system filters should be checked regularly to ensure that they are seated properly. Filters should be replaced on a routine schedule.

Protecting building occupants during building renovations or remodeling

The best strategy is to isolate the building area(s) undergoing renovations from occupied areas. Isolating the renovated area(s) usually means erecting barriers made of either plywood or polyethylene sheeting. Supply and return ducts should be covered in the area under renovation to prevent the spread of odors and construction dust. Air handling units serving areas under renovation should also be turned off if they serve only the area being renovated. Air handling units that are being serviced as part of the renovation should be locked out while they are being serviced. Ensure that the renovated area is under negative or neutral pressure in relation to adjacent occupied space. Evaluate work areas for potential harm to workers and relocate occupants as needed; prevent contamination from spreading to occupied areas.

When undertaking renovations that break the integrity of the building envelope, such as roofing work, regular checks should be made for water intrusions at the breaks in the envelope. Water damage and standing water should be cleaned up immediately.

Building Evaluation

You should look for and eliminate the source of moisture problems in the building. As stated earlier in this document, moisture problems can have many sources, including uncontrolled humidity, roof leaks, and landscaping or gutters that direct water into or under the building. Unvented combustion appliances and standing water following a flood are other sources. Also, you should remove all visible mold. Visible mold on external surfaces, especially on the walls of a building, may be an indicator of more severe contamination beneath the surface. However, mold removal without also the correction of the underlying water/moisture problem would not be effective since the mold would just grow back. If a greater problem is suspected, or a moisture problem has resulted in extensive fungal growth, an environmental investigation with emphasis on physical inspection is recommended (14). An experienced professional should be consulted to evaluate the situation and recommend or supervise the proper corrective action.

Selecting a qualified professional who can assist in providing a safe and healthful work environment

Occupational safety and health professionals are typically able to evaluate a building for mold, whereas occupational health care professionals are qualified to assess and treat illnesses and injuries.

OSHA Publication 3160, *The Occupational Health Professional's Services and Qualifications: Questions and Answers*, provides a thorough discussion of the roles of occupational health physicians, occupational health nurses, industrial hygienists, industrial engineers, safety professionals and other occupational health professionals (15). This document is available at: http://www.osha.gov/Publications/osha3160.pdf

Occupational physicians must have completed additional training in occupational medicine beyond the qualifications necessary for medical doctor or doctor of osteopathy licensure.

Physicians may be certified in the field after meeting rigorous qualifying standards and successfully completing the examination in occupational medicine given by the American Board of Preventive Medicine. The American College of Occupational and Environmental Medicine (www.acoem.org) maintains a directory of some 6,000 physicians and other health professionals specializing in occupational and environmental medicine. Your general practice physician may be able to refer you to a specialist from this list.

The American Industrial Hygiene Association (www.aiha.org) and the American Society of Safety Engineers (www.asse.org) maintain lists of consulting firms for occupational safety and health. Certified Industrial Hygienists (CIHs) and Certified Associate Industrial Hygienists (CAIHs) must have at least a bachelor's degree with a concentration in the sciences, have five years professional experience, and pass a rigorous certification examination. The American Board of Industrial Hygiene (www.abih.org) maintains a complete listing of all CIHs and CAIHs in good standing with the organization.

Certified Safety Professionals (CSPs) also must meet academic requirements, have at least four years of experience, and pass a rigorous certification examination. A roster of CSPs is maintained by the Board of Certified Safety Professionals (www.bcsp.com). Both CIHs and CSPs are required to attend continuing education courses to stay current in their field of practice.

Sampling for mold

Where visible mold is present, cleanup can proceed on the basis of the visual inspection. Sampling for molds and other bioaerosols is not usually necessary (1). There are currently no governmental or professional recommendations for airborne concentrations of mold, mold spores, mycotoxins, and other bioaerosols with which to compare any sampling results (16). However, sampling for mold may be considered in the following situations:

- When medical diagnosis is consistent with mold-associated illness;
- To delimit the outer boundaries of severely contaminated areas before and during a mold cleanup project; and

- After a cleanup, to show that the types and concentrations of mold in the area are similar to background levels (17).

Sampling for mold, mold spores, mycotoxins, and other bioaerosols are not part of a routine building evaluation.

Mold sampling strategies

Sampling and analysis of mold are complex and can become expensive. There is a lack of standard procedures for sampling and analysis (18). Sampling should be undertaken only after careful delineation of the sampling goals. For assistance with mold sampling, consult an experienced health and safety professional. Health and safety professionals, working closely with an accredited environmental microbiology laboratory, can determine and document the details concerning the necessary sampling strategy, including when and where to sample. Standardized methods, such as ACGIH, AIHA, NIOSH and OSHA methods, should be followed where available. Accredited laboratories that participate in the AIHA Environmental Microbiology Proficiency Analytical Testing (EMPAT) Program are listed on the AIHA website at http://www.aiha.org/LaboratoryServices/html/empat1.htm.

The meaning of mold sampling results that are in CFU/m² and CFU/m³

Sampling results for viable (living) microorganisms are presented as concentrations, and the units used will vary depending on the sample collection methods. Air sampling results are reported as colony-forming units per cubic meter of air (CFU/m³). Specialized sampling is reported in terms of the entity collected, i.e., if only spores were sampled, the results would be reported as spores/m³ (19). Bulk samples may be reported as colony-forming units per gram (CFU/g) of dust or material or colony-forming units per milliliter (CFU/ml) of stagnant water or slime (20). Wipe sample results are reported as colony-forming units per surface area such as CFU/m² or CFU/ft². These units represent the culturable portion of mold concentrations only and do not quantify the fragments and by-products of mold that may also exist.

Mold Control and Remediation

The purpose of mold remediation

The purpose of mold remediation is to identify and correct the water or moisture problem, remove or clean all contaminated materials, prevent the spread of contamination to other areas, and protect the health and safety of the building occupants. During any remediation, the health and safety of remediation workers must also be a priority. In every case of microbial contamination, including mold contamination, the underlying cause of the contamination must be rectified or the growth will recur (1).

These are the basic principles of mold remediation. For more thorough discussions of methods, recommendations, and remediation approaches for various levels of contamination, see OSHA's Safety and Health Information Bulletin entitled, "A Brief Guide to Mold in the Workplace" (SHIB 03-10-10), (1) which is available at: http://www.osha.gov/dts/shib/shib101003.html.

In particular, see discussions concerning:

- Additional measures for cleaning contaminated ductwork
- Biocides vs. antimicrobial agents
- Informing building occupants about mold remediation
- Informing remediation employees about the hazards of mold
- Personal protective equipment (PPE) for remediation employees.

Actions for Employees to Take

What to do about mold in the workplace

There are no standards that say how much mold is hazardous to your health. However, there should not be visible mold growth or objectionable moldy odors in your workplace. If you see or smell mold, or if you or others are experiencing mold-related health problems, report the problem to your employer so the problem can be investigated. If you believe that there is a mold hazard, you have the right to file a complaint with Federal OSHA or, in states with OSHA-approved state plans, the state occupational safety and health agency. You can contact your local Area Office of Federal OSHA or state occupational safety and health office or file a complaint online at http://www.osha.gov/as/opa/worker/complain.html. Links to the addresses and telephone numbers of the state occupational safety and health agency offices are available online at http://www.osha.gov/fso/osp/index.html. In addition, assistance with filing complaints, receiving workplace health and safety information and requesting OSHA publications, among other types of information, are available by calling OSHA's toll-free number at 1-800-321-6742.

Additional Help in Addressing Mold-Related Problems

Where to get more information

The following sources provide links to additional programs and information regarding mold:

Occupational Safety and Health Administration (OSHA) www.osha.gov Search "indoor air quality" or "molds and fungi" to link to sources of information related to Indoor Air Quality (IAQ) and mold.

Environmental Protection Agency (EPA)
www.epa.gov/iaq/pubs/

Indoor Air Quality Information Clearinghouse (IAQ Info)
1-800-438-4318
P.O. Box 37133
Washington, DC 20013-7133
e-mail: iaqinfo@aol.com

National Institute for Occupational Safety and Health (NIOSH)
www.cdc.gov/niosh   1-800-35-NIOSH (1-800-356-4674)
Education and Information Division
Publications Dissemination
4676 Columbia Parkway
Cincinnati, OH 45226-1988
e-mail: pubstaft@cdc.gov

International Facility Management Association
www.ifma.org   713-623-4362
1 E. Greenway Plaza, Suite 1100
Houston, TX 77046-0194

American Society of Heating, Refrigerating, and Air-Conditioning
Engineers (ASHRAE)
www.ashrae.org   1-800-527-4723
1791 Tullie Circle, N.E.
Atlanta, GA 30329

Methods

Relevant publications used as references for this document were located through a PubMed (National Library of Medicine) search. PubMed was selected because of its broad scope of publications: Medline (National Library of Medicine), other life sciences journals, and links to sites providing full-text articles. Key words used to execute the search included mold, epidemiology, BRI, hypersensitivity pneumonitis, farmer's lung, air conditioner or humidifier lung, mycotoxins, and respiratory illness.

The size of the search results was managed, where appropriate, by limiting searches to the English language and human studies. Single word and Boolean logic operators (AND, OR, and NOT) were used to link words and phrases for more precise searches which yielded summary abstracts (from a choice of display formats). Search summaries were quickly reviewed and further refined for useable selections. Articles were obtained either directly from online sources or through the OSHA Technical Data System and were reviewed both by OSHA staff and contractors.

Similar searches of the OSHA IAQ Docket (H-122) were made through the Intra–OSHA Document Management System (DMS). This system contains the entire IAQ docket in a format that allows full-text selection of documents and returns a list of exhibit numbers that contain the term(s) of interest, which can then be viewed for usefulness and retrieved as desired.

Articles were chosen for their subject matter and relevance to workplace building-related illness and were reviewed by OSHA and its contractors. Not all papers reviewed were utilized.

Appendix

Molds can cause three types of adverse health effects in humans; allergy, infection, and toxin-mediated conditions. These adverse health effects are discussed in more detail below.

Allergy

Allergic rhinitis

Allergic rhinitis has several signs and symptoms. The symptoms of allergic rhinitis include sneezing; itchy eyes, nose, and throat; a stuffy or runny nose; sore throat; cough; watery eyes; headache; and fatigue. These symptoms may be worse in indoor environments and may peak in hot and humid seasons. Common physical findings include red or bloodshot eyes, a runny nose, watery eyes, and thickened nasal mucous membranes. Multiple airborne allergens other than molds (e.g., pollens, animal dander, and dust mites) may be involved. However, when a person is also sensitized to mold, an indoor environment contaminated with mold spores may aggravate the signs and symptoms of allergic rhinitis (18).

Allergic asthma

Allergic asthma is a chronic lung disease that is caused by breathing in substances known to be allergens (sensitizers). Asthma occurs when the airways become inflamed and the surrounding muscles tighten and contract. Asthma causes breathing difficulties by making it harder for air to flow in and out of the lungs. Symptoms of asthma include tightness of the chest, shortness of breath, coughing, and wheezing (21). Although a complete patient history and physical exam are the most important methods employed to diagnose asthma, chest X-rays, pulmonary function testing, and immunologic studies occasionally are also used.

Exposure to mold clearly plays a role in asthma. Molds produce a large variety of compounds that are potentially allergenic (e.g., proteins). Potency varies among these allergens. The epidemi-

ological evidence from well-conducted studies documents the sensitizing potential of mold allergens. Also, well-documented evidence indicates that fungal sensitization is related to asthma (22).

Hypersensitivity pneumonitis (HP)

HP (or extrinsic allergic alveolitis) refers to a group of allergic lung diseases caused by the inhalation of antigens contained in a wide variety of organic dusts. Antigens are substances that provoke an allergic reaction (i.e., an immune response with the formation of antibodies) when introduced into the body. HP occurs when very small antigenic particles (5 micrometers or less in diameter and invisible to the naked eye) penetrate into the deepest areas of the lungs (the alveoli) and cause inflammation. HP may occur as an acute, subacute, or chronic condition. Symptoms and signs of the acute form may occur 4-6 hours after significant antigen exposure and include chest tightness, difficulty breathing, fever, chills, cough, and muscle aches (5, 23). If exposure to the antigen is repeated frequently, scars can form on the lungs, resulting in a disabling condition known as fibrosis (23, 24). Symptoms and signs associated with the subacute and chronic forms of the disease include cough, shortness of breath, fatigue, and weight loss (23).

A variety of organic dust sources may cause HP. The causative agents may include bacteria, fungi, animal proteins, insects, and chemicals. The numerous clinical syndromes are generally given names reflecting the circumstances or sources of exposure. For example, farmer's lung results from exposures to moldy hay, straw, grain, and compost. Pigeon breeder's or bird-fancier's disease/lung results from exposures to avian protein in bird dander, feathers, and droppings. Although HP is not commonly reported as a BRI, sources of concern for building owners and managers include molds, bacteria, and other organisms growing in heating, ventilating, and air conditioning systems, humidifiers, and water-damaged buildings. To a lesser extent, HP may be associated with exposure to birds or bird droppings during building cleaning and maintenance activities.

Ventilation pneumonitis

Ventilation pneumonitis (also called air-conditioner lung, humidifier lung, and humidifier fever) is hypersensitivity pneumonitis (HP) that is due to fungal and microbial growth in ventilation and air conditioning systems. Onset can occur when maintenance work is performed on these systems. Diagnosis is based on a combination of characteristic symptoms, chest X-ray findings, pulmonary function abnormalities, and sometimes immunologic study findings. Inspection of the heating, ventilation, and air conditioning (HVAC) systems and confirmation of the diagnoses are more useful than sampling for mold (8, 25).

How HP differs from asthma

HP differs from asthma in several ways including pathology, diagnosis, and treatment. For example, HP differs from asthma in the location of the inflammation. Asthma is characterized by inflammation of the larger airways close to the mouth and nose. HP is characterized by inflammation of the smallest airways (bronchioles) and the air sacs (alveoli) (24).

Infection

Systemic fungal infections

Histoplasmosis and cryptococcosis are examples of infections caused by fungi (*Histoplasma capsulatum* and *Cryptococcus neoformans*, respectively). The main source of exposure to both organisms is debris around bird roosts and soil contaminated with bird and bat droppings. Concern about health risks may be warranted in situations where there is a significant accumulation of bird or bat droppings near ventilation systems and in attics. Both infections are primarily seen in immunocompromised individuals such as those with AIDS, but can also occur in normal healthy individuals (26, 27, 28).

Toxin-Mediated Conditions

Mycotoxins

Mycotoxins are metabolic by-products produced by some molds that can cause toxic reactions in humans or animals. Some mycotoxins are concentrated on or within mold spores (3). Mycotoxins may be hazardous through ingestion, inhalation, or skin contact (29). The most well-known and studied mycotoxin is aflatoxin. Although not included within the scope of this document, aflatoxin is one of the most potent liver carcinogens known and has been found on contaminated peanuts, grains, and other human and animal foodstuffs (3).

A wide variety of molds, even some of the most commonly found molds that are generally considered harmless, are capable of producing mycotoxins (30). Some molds can produce several mycotoxins (3). Mycotoxin production varies widely depending on the species and growth conditions, such as availability of nutrients, the suitability of the surface on which growth can take place, environmental factors (e.g., relative humidity, temperature, light, oxygen, and carbon dioxide), the season, maturity of the fungal colony, and competition with other microorganisms (12, 15).

The presence of mycotoxin-producing mold in a building does not necessarily mean that mycotoxins are present or that building occupants have been exposed to mycotoxins (3, 12, 15). Mycotoxins are generally not volatile (i.e., do not become airborne easily), and according to recent studies, mycotoxins have not been shown to cause health problems for occupants at concentrations usually seen in residential or commercial buildings (12, 29, 31).

Adverse health effects that may be due in part to mycotoxins have been reported to occur among agricultural workers. However, these effects are due to the inhalation of very high levels of molds (e.g., in silage and spoiled grain products) that are orders of magnitude greater than the typical exposures that might be seen when mold is found growing in the indoor environment (29).

Toxic mold

The phrase "toxic mold" has been used by journalists and many others to refer to molds that have been implicated in severe health effects in humans. Although not a scientific term, it is typically used in the press to refer to those molds capable of producing mycotoxins and incorrectly implies that these molds are more dangerous than others. In fact, all molds under the right conditions have the potential to cause allergic reactions, infections, and toxin-mediated conditions (32).

Individuals who believe that they are suffering from mold-related symptoms should seek medical attention. Although there is no singular medical specialty that addresses the indoor air environment, an occupational medicine physician has specialty training addressing diseases associated with the work environment.

See page 12 of this document for assistance in selecting a qualified professional, including a health care professional.

References

1. U.S. Department of Labor. Occupational Safety and Health Administration (OSHA). 2003. "A Brief Guide to Mold in the Workplace." Safety and Health Information Bulletin (SHIB 03-10-10). Available online at http://www.osha.gov/dts/shib/shib101003.html

2. Burge, H.A. (ed.). 1995. *Bioaersols (Indoor Air Research Series).* Boca Raton: CRC Press, Inc.

3. U.S. Environmental Protection Agency (EPA). 2001. "Mold Remediation in Schools and Commercial Buildings." Office of Air and Radiation, Indoor Environments Division. Document Number EPA 402-K-01-001, March 2001. Available online at http://www.epa.gov/iaq/molds/graphics/moldremediation.pdf

4. Morbidity and Mortality Weekly Report (MMWR). 2000. "Update: Pulmonary Hemorrhage/Hemosiderosis Among Infants – Cleveland, Ohio, 1993-1996." MMWR, 49(09):180-184, March 10, 2000 (Note: Also see Errata: 49(10):213, March 17, 2000).

5. California Department of Health Services (CDHS), 2001. "Molds in Indoor Workplaces." Hazard Evaluation System & Information Service (HESIS), CDHS, Occupational Health Branch. March 2001. Available online at http://www.dhs.cahwnet.gov/ohb/HESIS/molds.pdf

6. American Industrial Hygiene Association (AIHA). 2002. "The Facts About Mold." Available online at www.aiha.org/GovernmentAffairs-PR/html/oomold.htm

7. Mendell, M.J., et al. 2002. "Improving the Health of Workers in Indoor Environments: Priority Research Needs for a National Occupational Research Agenda." American Journal of Public Health, 92(9):1430-1440.

8. U.S. Environmental Protection Agency (EPA). 1991. "Building Air Quality: A Guide for Building Owners and Facility Managers." Office of Air and Radiation, Indoor Air Division and U.S. Department of Health and Human Services, Public Health Service, National Institute for Occupational Safety and Health. December

1991. Available online at http://www.epa.gov/iaq/largebldgs/baqtoc.html

9. Rafferty, P.J. (ed.). 1993. "The Industrial Hygienist's Guide to Indoor Air Quality Investigations." The American Industrial Hygiene Association (AIHA). Technical Committee on Indoor Air Quality.

10. Pope, A.M., Patterson, R. and Burge, H. (eds.). 1993. "Indoor Allergens: Assessing and Controlling Adverse Health Effects." Committee on the Health Effects of Indoor Allergens. Division of Health Promotion and Disease Prevention. Institute of Medicine. Washington, DC: National Academy Press. Available online at http://books.nap.edu/catalog/2056.html

11. Morey, P.R. and Singh, J. 1991. "Indoor Air Quality in Nonindustrial Occupational Environments." In: Clayton, G.D. and Clayton, F.E. (eds.). 1991. *Patty's Industrial Hygiene and Toxicology*, 4th Edition, Volume I, Part A. New York: John Wiley and Sons, Inc., pp. 531-594.

12. American College of Occupational and Environmental Medicine (ACOEM). 2002. "Adverse Human Health Effects Associated with Molds in the Indoor Environment." ACOEM Evidence-based Statement, October 27, 2002.

13. U.S. Environmental Protection Agency (EPA). 1997. "Should You Have the Air Ducts in Your Home Cleaned?" Office of Air and Radiation, Indoor Environments Division. Document Number EPA-402-K-97-002, October 1997. Available online at http://www.epa.gov/iaq/pubs/airduct.html

14. Fung, F. and Hughson, W.G. 2003. "Health Effects of Indoor Fungal Bioaerosol Exposure." Applied Occupational and Environmental Hygiene, 18(7):535-544.

15. U.S. Department of Labor, Occupational Safety and Health Administration (OSHA). 1999. "The Occupational Health Professional's Services and Qualifications: Questions and Answers." OSHA 3160, 1999 (revised). Available online at http://www.osha.gov/ Publications/osha3160.pdf

16. Mahoney, D.P. and Spear, J.E. 2003. "Mold Risk Assessment & Remediation." Professional Safety. August 2003, pp. 20-26.

17. Macher, J. (ed.). 1999. *Bioaerosols – Assessment and Control.* American Conference of Governmental Industrial Hygienists (ACGIH). Cincinnati, OH.

18. Arora, A.S. 2003. "Understanding the Health Effects of Mold." Guest Column. The AIH Diplomate, Fall 2003, Issue #03-3, pp. vi – vii. Available online at http://www.aiha.org/TheAcademy/documents/Diplo03-3.pdf

19. Ness, S.A. 1991. *Air Monitoring for Toxic Exposures – An Integrated Approach.* New York: Van Nostrand Reinhold.

20. U.S. Department of Labor, Occupational Safety and Health Administration (OSHA). 1999. "Indoor Air Quality Investigation." OSHA Technical Manual, Directive Number TED 1-0.15A, Section III: Chapter 2, January 20, 1999. Available online at http://www.osha.gov/dts/osta/otm_iii/otm_iii_2.html

21. Queensland Government. 2000. "Occupational Asthma - Worker Guide." Department of Industrial Relations, Division of Workplace Health and Safety, Queensland, Australia, October 2000. Available online at http://www.whs.qld.gov.au/guide/gde52.pdf

22. Institute of Medicine. 2000. *Clearing the Air: Asthma and Indoor Exposures.* National Academy Press, Washington, DC. pp. 158-175.

23. Fink, J. 1986. "Hypersensitivity Pneumonitis." In: Merchant, J.A. (ed.). *Occupational Respiratory Diseases,* U.S. Department of Health and Human Services (DHHS), Public Health Service, National Institute for Occupational Safety and Health (NIOSH). DHHS (NIOSH) Publication No. 86-102, September 1986. pp. 481-529. Available online at http://www.cdc.gov/niosh/86-102.html

24. Levy, B.S. and Wegman, D.H. 1995. (eds.). *Occupational Health: Recognizing and Preventing Work-Related Disease and Injury.* 3rd Edition. Boston: Little Brown and Company.

25. Bierbaum, P.J. 1989. Testimony before the Subcommittee on Natural Resources, Agriculture Research, and Environment,

OSHA
www.osha.gov

Committee on Science, Space and Technology, U.S. House of Representatives, September 27, 1989, OSHA IAQ Docket, H-122 (Ex. 3-1160E).

26. National Institute for Occupational Safety and Health (NIOSH). 1997. "Histoplasmosis: Protecting Workers at Risk." U.S. Department of Health and Human Services (DHHS), Public Health Service, Centers for Disease Control and Prevention, NIOSH, National Center for Infectious Diseases. Publication No. DHHS (NIOSH) 97-146, September 1997. Available online at http://www.cdc.gov/niosh/97-146.html

27. Centers for Disease Control and Prevention (CDC). 2002. "Cryptococcosis." CDC, National Center for Infectious Diseases. Available online at http://www.cdc.gov/ncidod/dbmd/diseaseinfo/cryptococcosis_t.htm

28. Perfect, J.R. and Casadevall, A. 2002. "Cryptococcosis." Infectious Disease Clinics of North America. 16(4):837-74.

29. Robbins, C.A., Swenson, L.J., Nealley, M.L., Gots, R.E., and Kelman, B.J. 2000. "Health Effects of Mycotoxins in Indoor Air: A Critical Review." Applied Occupational and Environmental Hygiene, 15(10):773-784.

30. Gots, R.E., 2001. "Mold and Mold Toxins: The Newest Toxic Tort." Journal of Controversial Medical Claims, Vol. 8, No. 1, February 2001.

31. Page, E.H. and Trout, D.B. 2001. "The Role of *Stachybotrys* Mycotoxins in Building-Related Illness." American Industrial Hygiene Association Journal, 62:644-648.

32. Davis, P.J. 2001. "Molds, Toxic Molds, and Indoor Air Quality." California Research Bureau (CRB), California State Library, Sacramento, CA. CRB Note. Vol. 8, No.1, March 2001. Available online at http://www.library.ca.gov/crb/01/notes/v8n1.pdf

OSHA Assistance

OSHA can provide extensive help through a variety of programs, including technical assistance about effective safety and health programs, state plans, workplace consultations, voluntary protection programs, strategic partnerships, training and education, and more. An overall commitment to workplace safety and health can add value to your business, to your workplace and to your life.

Safety and Health Program Management Guidelines

Effective management of worker safety and health protection is a decisive factor in reducing the extent and severity of work-related injuries and illnesses and their related costs. To assist employers and employees in developing effective safety and health programs, OSHA published recommended Safety and Health Program Management Guidelines (54 Federal Register 3904-3916, January 26, 1989). These voluntary guidelines apply to all places of employment covered by OSHA.

The guidelines identify four general elements that are critical to the development of a successful safety and health management program:

Management leadership and employee involvement;

Work analysis;

Hazard prevention and control; and

Safety and health training.

The guidelines recommend specific actions under each of these general elements to achieve an effective safety and health program. The guidelines can be viewed on OSHA's website at www.osha.gov/safetyhealth/standards.html under the heading Federal Registers.

State Programs

The *Occupational Safety and Health Act of 1970* (OSH Act) encourages states to develop and operate their own job safety and health plans. States with plans approved by OSHA under section

27

18(b) of the OSH Act must adopt standards and enforce requirements that are at least as effective as federal requirements. There are currently 26 state plan states: 22 of these administer plans covering both private and public (state and local government) employees; the other plans, Connecticut, New Jersey, New York and the Virgin Islands, cover public sector employees only.

Consultation Services

Consultation assistance is available on request to employers who want help in establishing and maintaining a safe and healthful workplace. Largely funded by OSHA, the service is provided at no cost to the employer. Primarily developed for smaller employers with more hazardous operations, the consultation service is delivered by state governments employing professional safety and health consultants. Comprehensive assistance includes an appraisal of all mechanical systems, work practices and occupational safety and health hazards of the workplace and all aspects of the employer's present job safety and health program.

The program is separate from OSHA's inspection efforts. No penalties are proposed or citations issued for hazards identified by the consultant. The service is confidential. For more information concerning consultation assistance, see the OSHA website at www.osha.gov/dcsp/smallbusiness/consult.html.

Voluntary Protection Programs

Voluntary Protection Programs (VPPs) and onsite consultation services, when coupled with an effective enforcement program, expand worker protection to help meet the goals of the OSH Act. The three levels of VPP—Star, Merit, and Star Demonstration—are designed to recognize outstanding achievement by companies that have successfully incorporated comprehensive safety and health programs into their total management system. The VPPs motivate others to achieve excellent safety and health results in the same outstanding way as they establish a cooperative relationship among employers, employees and OSHA.

For additional information on VPPs and how to apply, visit OSHA's website at: www.osha.gov/dcsp/vpp/index.html or contact your nearest OSHA Area or Regional Office listed at the end of this publication.

Strategic Partnership Program

OSHA's Strategic Partnership Program, the newest of OSHA's cooperative programs, helps encourage, assist and recognize the efforts of partners to eliminate serious workplace hazards and achieve a high level of worker safety and health. Whereas OSHA's Consultation Program and VPP entail one-on-one relationships between OSHA and individual worksites, most strategic partnerships seek to have a broader impact by building cooperative relationships with groups of employers and employees. These partnerships are voluntary, cooperative relationships between OSHA, employers, employee representatives and others (e.g., labor unions, trade and professional associations, universities and other government agencies). For more information on this and other cooperative programs, contact your nearest OSHA office, or visit OSHA's website at www.osha.gov

Alliance Programs

The Alliances Program enables organizations committed to workplace safety and health to collaborate with OSHA to prevent injuries and illnesses in the workplace. OSHA and the Alliance participants work together to reach out to, educate and lead the nation's employers and their employees in improving and advancing workplace safety and health.

Groups that can form an Alliance with OSHA include employers, labor unions, trade or professional groups, educational institutions and government agencies. In some cases, organizations may be building on existing relationships with OSHA through other cooperative programs.

There are few formal program requirements for Alliances and the agreements do not include an enforcement component. However, OSHA and the participating organizations must define, implement and meet a set of short- and long-term goals that fall into three

categories: training and education; outreach and communication; and promoting the national dialogue on workplace safety and health.

Training and Education

OSHA's area offices offer a variety of information services, such as compliance assistance, publications, audiovisual aids, technical advice, and speakers for special engagements.

OSHA's Training Institute in Arlington Heights, IL, provides basic and advanced courses in safety and health for federal and state compliance officers, state consultants, federal agency personnel and private sector employers, employees and their representatives.

The OSHA Training Institute also has established OSHA Training Institute Education Centers to address the increased demand for its courses from the private sector and from other federal agencies (see OSHA's website at: www.osha.gov/fso/ote/training/edcenters/index.html). These centers are nonprofit colleges, universities and other organizations that have been selected after a competition for participation in the program.

OSHA also provides funds to nonprofit organizations, through grants, to conduct workplace training and education in subjects where OSHA believes there is a lack of workplace training.

Grants are awarded annually. Grant recipients are expected to contribute 20 percent of the total grant cost.

For more information on grants, training and education, contact the OSHA Training Institute, Office of Training and Education, on OSHA's website at: www.osha.gov/dcsp/ote/index.html, or at 2020 South Arlington Heights Road, Arlington Heights, IL 60005-4102, (847) 297-4810, Fax (847) 297-4874. For further information on any OSHA program, contact your nearest OSHA area or regional office listed at the end of this publication.

Information Available Electronically

OSHA has a variety of materials and tools available on its website at www.osha.gov. These include e-Tools such as Expert Advisors, Electronic Compliance Assistance Tools (e-cats), Technical Links; regulations, directives and publications; videos

and other information for employers and employees. OSHA's software programs and compliance assistance tools walk you through challenging safety and health issues and common problems to find the best solutions for your workplace.

A wide variety of OSHA materials, including standards, interpretations, directives, and more, can be purchased on CD-ROM from the U.S. Government Printing Office, Superintendent of Documents, phone toll-free (866) 512-1800.

OSHA Publications

OSHA has an extensive publications program. For a listing of free or sales items, visit OSHA's website at www.osha.gov or contact the OSHA Publications Office, U.S. Department of Labor, 200 Constitution Avenue, NW, N-3101, Washington, DC 20210. Telephone (202) 693-1888 or fax to (202) 693-2498.

Contacting OSHA

To report an emergency, file a complaint or seek OSHA advice, assistance or products, call (800) 321-OSHA or contact your nearest OSHA regional or area office listed below. The teletypewriter (TTY) number is (877) 889-5627.

You can also file a complaint online and obtain more information on OSHA federal and state programs by visiting OSHA's website at www.osha.gov.

For further information on any OSHA program, contact your nearest OSHA area or regional office listed at the end of this publication.

OSHA

www.osha.gov

OSHA Regional Offices

Region I
(CT,* ME, MA, NH, RI, VT*)
JFK Federal Building, Room E340
Boston, MA 02203
(617) 565-9860

Region II
(NJ,* NY,* PR,* VI*)
201 Varick Street, Room 670
New York, NY 10014
(212) 337-2378

Region III
(DE, DC, MD,* PA, VA,* WV)
The Curtis Center
170 S. Independence Mall West
Suite 740 West
Philadelphia, PA 19106-3309
(215) 861-4900

Region IV
(AL, FL, GA, KY,* MS, NC,* SC,* TN*)
61 Forsyth Street, SW
Atlanta, GA 30303
(404) 562-2300

Region V
(IL, IN,* MI,* MN,* OH, WI)
230 South Dearborn Street
Room 3244
Chicago, IL 60604
(312) 353-2220

Region VI
(AR, LA, NM,* OK, TX)
525 Griffin Street, Room 602
Dallas, TX 75202
(214) 767-4731 or 4736 x224

Region VII
(IA,* KS, MO, NE)
City Center Square
1100 Main Street, Suite 800
Kansas City, MO 64105
(816) 426-5861

Region VIII
(CO, MT, ND, SD, UT,* WY*)
1999 Broadway, Suite 1690
PO Box 46550
Denver, CO 80202-5716
(720) 264-6550

Region IX
(American Samoa, AZ,* CA,* HI,* NV,*
Northern Mariana Islands)
71 Stevenson Street, Room 420
San Francisco, CA 94105
(415) 975-4310

Region X
(AK,* ID, OR,* WA*)
1111 Third Avenue, Suite 715
Seattle, WA 98101-3212
(206) 553-5930

* These 26 states and territories operate their own OSHA-approved job safety and health programs (Connecticut, New Jersey, New York and the Virgin Islands plans cover public employees only). States with approved programs must have standards that are identical to, or at least as effective as, the Federal OSHA standards.

Note: To get contact information for OSHA Area Offices, OSHA-approved State Plans and OSHA Consultation Projects, please visit us online at www.osha.gov or call us at 1-800-321-OSHA.